Darrel Johnson is a walking miracle. Not only were there many times in his life when he should have been killed, but he is currently battling stage 4 pancreatic cancer. Growing up, he used to question how he managed to stay alive. Now, he knows that it is by God's grace that he has survived. *ALL THINGS – From The Streets To the Pulpit* is Johnson's powerful testimony to share his story with the masses and encourage all to have faith in God and trust Him to perform miracles in their own lives.

**Xulon Editorial Review**

# ALL THINGS FROM THE STREETS to the PULPIT

*Memoirs of What God Did and How He Did It!*

DARREL JOHNSON

XULON PRESS

Xulon Press
555 Winderley Pl, Suite 225
Maitland, FL 32751
407.339.4217
www.xulonpress.com

© 2023 by Darrel Johnson

All rights reserved solely by the author. The author guarantees all contents are original and do not infringe upon the legal rights of any other person or work. No part of this book may be reproduced in any form without the permission of the author.

Due to the changing nature of the Internet, if there are any web addresses, links, or URLs included in this manuscript, these may have been altered and may no longer be accessible. The views and opinions shared in this book belong solely to the author and do not necessarily reflect those of the publisher. The publisher therefore disclaims responsibility for the views or opinions expressed within the work.

Unless otherwise indicated, Scripture quotations taken from the King James Version (KJV) – *public domain.*

Scripture quotations taken from the Holy Bible, New International Version (NIV). Copyright © 1973, 1978, 1984, 2011 by Biblica, Inc.™. Used by permission. All rights reserved.

Scripture quotations taken from The Message (MSG). Copyright © 1993, 1994, 1995, 1996, 2000, 2001, 2002. Used by permission of NavPress Publishing Group. Used by permission. All rights reserved.

Scripture quotations taken from the New King James Version (NKJV). Copyright © 1982 by Thomas Nelson, Inc. Used by permission. All rights reserved.

Paperback ISBN-13: 978-1-66288-338-5
Hard Cover ISBN-13: 978-1-66288-339-2
Ebook ISBN-13: 978-1-66288-340-8

# Introduction

To the reader. Please keep this scripture attached subliminally to your thoughts as you read through this book.

*And we know that all things work together for good to them that love God, to them who are the called according to his purpose.*
*Romans 8:28 (KJV)*

Been there, done that. There was a song my mom used to like. "That's Life." I've heard it sung by many different entertainers. She liked to play the version sung by Frank Sinatra. Some of the lyrics to that song went something like this. "I've been a puppet, a poet, a pirate, a pauper, a pawn, and a king. I've been up and down and over and out, and I know one thing. Each time I find myself lying flat on my face, I pick myself up and get back in the race."[1]

When I juxtapose the picture that I see of my life to the lyrics of that song, these thoughts often come together in my mind. I have literally started my life over three times. I have done fairly during some times and poorly in others. I have lived and experienced things that most people should never see, live, or experience. I have been to places and done things that most people only

---

[1] Sinatra, Frank. That's Life. Capitol Records,1963 https://genius.com/Frank-sinatra-thats-life-lyrics

dream of going to or doing themselves. I've done some things that people should never do. Doctors, on two separate occasions, told my family that I might not make it through the night. On one occasion, I was told that I should not have made it to the hospital, but should have died or passed out on the street days earlier.

In spite of all this, I've led a truly blessed life. God has been there all along, fulfilling His plan, preparing me, molding me, and using me. I just didn't see it most of the time. On the brighter side, I've always had an entrepreneurial spirit. Despite very little formal business training, I always managed to do well and support myself financially. I've lived quite comfortably. There's a certain level of success in everything I set my hand to. I just didn't set my goals very high. I've owned two separate welding businesses, each of which was minimally functional and self-supporting for at least three years. I've partnered in a gas station, an auto repair business with my family, a photo processing laboratory, and a store.

In the middle of all of that, I gained advanced certifications in welding, became a licensed insurance sales agent, achieved a level of third-degree Master Mason, and achieved the appendant degrees to the 32nd degree of the Ancient Accepted Scottish Rite of Freemasonry in the class of 2015. The class photo is depicted on the last page of my book and hangs on the wall in the Scottish Right Hall in Maryland alongside most of the founding fathers of this country, including George Washington himself. I remember on graduation day roaming the room looking at the class photos of all of the famous historical figures of American history mounted on the walls and finding myself on the same walls in the same room where they stood. I was in total awe at what God had done thus far.

In addition to the Maryland Council of Select Master's Super Excellent Master's Degree, I became a leader in multiple churches, including earning the titles of minister, reverend, and pastor. I've achieved many certificates and awards in these areas and became a PADI certified advanced open water scuba diver. I've jumped out of a perfectly good airplane skydiving two miles above the earth and experienced the thrill of riding motorcycles at speeds of 180 miles per hour. For the last ten years, I've been operating a successful home inspection business, the Johnson Team LLC. I guess you could say I finally learned to stop being crazy, get it right, fully legitimate, and above board. Summing it up without going into any great details, I've been a police officer, a home improvement contractor, a criminal, a leader in society, a drug dealer, a drug addict, a thief, a charity benefactor, a teacher, a preacher, and a violent offender along with a thug and vigilante.

God has been there, fully involved, through every step of the process. My hopes are that those who read this book will come to understand how sovereign God really is to every life and especially the life of this Black man. We can't continue to limit God to any one religious belief structure or group of doctrinal interpretations. We must see God in all creation, every man, woman, child, animal, beast, plant, and creature. I wish to help nurture the development of a more spiritual relationship and less religious one in every reader. There is a piece of you in this book. I'm sure that you will find stories that you will identify with and emotions that you will share.

I take you back to the verse at the beginning of this chapter. *And we know that all things work together for good to them that love God to them who are the called according to his purpose* (Rom. 8:28 KJV). The operative word being "all" is a powerful word. Look at God.

In this book, between some of the chapters you will find inserts that I call" Nuggets." Some of them I wrote and some I've collected through the years and I'm not quite sure where they originated. They are simply things for the readers to ponder on.

## Nugget

"I put no stock in religion. By the word religion, I have seen the lunacy of fanatics of every denomination be called the will of God. Holiness is in right action, and courage on behalf of those who cannot defend themselves, and goodness. What God desires is here [the head] and here [the heart] and what you decide to do every day will make you a good man… or not." [2]

William Monahan, *Kingdom of Heaven*

---

[2] Monahan, William, Kingdom Of Heaven, The movie (https://www.reddit.com/r/Stoicism/comments/3qh4l5/quote_of_the_day_6_holiness_is_in_right_action/)

# Chapter 1

When I was a small child, my mom and dad took a picture of me doing something that I later realized was the beginning of the development, or the expression of the person that I was becoming. That one picture and the story that she told me about it clearly explained my thinking patterns at that time and many of the behavioral characteristics that I carry with me to this day. The picture was a picture of me as a toddler. I don't know exactly how old I was, maybe four years or so. I had a little red wagon in tow, and in it was a stack of books and a pair of rubber boots. The story that she told me on different occasions throughout my life about this picture goes as follows.

You packed your boots, some books, and a few other things in a little red wagon and announced to them that I was running away from home and that I didn't want to live there anymore. My parents thought it was very funny, so they agreed just to see where I would go with it. She said that I walked to the corner, stood at the crosswalk for quite some time, looked around, then clearly made the decision that it was a bad idea and came back home. Somewhere in the process, I must have realized that it was a bad idea, so I returned home, went back to the drawing board, and developed a new plan. I've heard that story many times since then. Usually, it was in the middle of a life-changing event, trial, or new venture that I was entering into. Once when I was around twelve,

I remember running away again. That time, it lasted for almost three days.

Let me take a moment to give you more of a background picture of the atmosphere in the neighborhood that I grew up in. My family, in my estimation or compared to most of the friends and family I had in my neighborhood, were upper middle class. My parents had decent jobs, a blue-collar worker and a barmaid. We lived in a three-bedroom house and had two cars. There was a lot of love, a lot of family, and a lot of good relationships. As with any family, there were also skeletons in the closet and bad things that happened behind the scenes. I lived half a block from the infamous 40 Projects. Public School #40 sat at the corner of 109th Avenue and Union Hall Street. It was quite common to hear of and find body parts in the incinerator shafts of the project buildings and drug addicts overdosing lying on the park benches where we played. There existed an unwritten rule in the streets. Small children and old folks were always guarded and protected by and from the bad things. Anyway, this is where I grew up. I slept in those project halls for three nights that time when I ran away. My dad had ordered my family not to look for me. His way of teaching me a lesson. Overall, I was happy and well-adjusted considering the realities. And more blessed than most.

One of the gifts that God blessed me with is a high level of discernment. Of course, I didn't know what that was as a child, but I did understand things that I could not say to adults or most people. For example, I could usually tell when I was being lied to or manipulated, and I could see through adults in ways that I could not express. The neighborhood we grew up in was South Jamaica, Queens, nicknamed "40 Projects." It had a reputation that spread across every urban housing complex in the five boroughs that had bad reputations. Even the drug addicts who were shooting up on the park benches would chase small children away and hide their bad habits from them, protecting them from seeing the negative things that were all around them. It was a time when, at ten years old, I was allowed to get on the New York City subway and take the train into Manhattan to go to my dentist appointments by myself. My dentist's office was around the corner from Bryant Park, right near Times Square. At that time in New York City, no children should have been allowed near Bryant Park without parental supervision. My mother would give me change and a note telling me that if I ran into any trouble or got lost to find a police officer, tell them my address, and tell them I was lost. They would give me directions to get home. Or I was to find a phone booth and call home.

I quite enjoyed the freedom and got lost regularly. I came to know my way around four of the five boroughs by subway and bus like I knew the back of my hand. I used to ride all day. Sometimes, I got in trouble for coming home four or five hours after my dentist appointment was over. I would usually find my mom sitting there worrying. She began to call me her prodigal son. It wasn't until I was in my twenties before I even learned what that meant. Nor did I care. I've never been afraid to venture out and explore. It was my nature and I quite enjoyed it. I also can't remember having any feelings of fear, more of amazement and excitement every time I learned about new places and new things. My inquisitive nature caused me to take everything apart and study it. I very rarely asked for assistance. I would just wander around until I found my way. Hindsight being what they call 20/20 vision. Jesus was with me all along.

Childhood in the sixties and seventies was quite different to what it is now, especially when it came to disciplining children. I don't know about every culture, but I do know that in the African

American culture in my neighborhood, you could come home and get a beating, spanking, whipping, or put on punishment as different methods of discipline. In my home, discipline was often what would be considered, by today's standards, abuse. My dad disciplined us the way his parents disciplined him. And his parents disciplined him the way his grandparents disciplined them. Imagine that we weren't very far from the way slaves were treated. Getting whipped and beaten very violently. I'll give you some examples.

When I was very young, my father bought me a guitar as a birthday gift. I really love music. I always have and always will. I remember sitting on the floor, leaning against the closet in my living room, plucking at the strings and playing with that guitar all day. Learning how to adjust the tension on the strings to change the tones that came from each pluck of string, pressing against the strings on different areas, and learning the different sounds. And of course, experimenting like tightening the strings too tight until they eventually popped. No big deal at the time, as long as I had more strings left to pluck on and continue playing. By the time my father got home, I was down to three strings and still sitting on the floor against the closet playing my guitar. When he saw the broken strings, he immediately snatched the guitar from my hand in a rage about how I broke another thing that he bought me. He hit me over the head with the back of the guitar, cracking it along the body of the guitar. I kept that guitar, but never played it again.

On many occasions, my father would walk up to my brother or myself and punch, slap, or hit us in some way, form, or fashion, usually hard enough to knock us down, for something that we had done days earlier or on another occasion. Or at another thing that he was just getting around to the beating for. Once I built a bridge out of toothpicks that I thought would be quite fun to blow up, like the scene from the movie *The Bridge on the River Kwai*. I rigged it with firecrackers on the dining room shelf. I tried to wire them so that they would blow up simultaneously and I lit the fuse… What a mess. Of course, he came home, and it was time for the beating.

On this occasion, he decided to teach me not to play with fire and matches. I had Lee jeans and Lee jacket to match. It had pockets all over the place. He sat on me, holding me down on top of a hassock, which used to sit in my dining room. He stuffed my pockets with toilet tissue and proceeded to tell me if I wanted to play with matches, then I would see what it was like to get burned. Then he started lighting the different wads of toilet tissue hanging out of my pocket. I didn't really get burned at that time, but the trauma of having a 200-plus pound man retaining me by sitting on my less than one-hundred-pound body still sticks with me today. It's like a mild form of claustrophobia. If you strap me down or tie me into a situation where I can't move, I'm gonna flip out.

His violent streaks were extreme. I could always count on my mother's voice to scream "Allen!" whenever he went a little too far. An example of too far was when he lit the matches. On another occasion, he threw me from the doorway in the living room through the dining room. Where I landed was on the kitchen floor at the doorway. A scuff mark from one of my shoes was on the ceiling in the middle of the dining room. It stayed there for many years. Without going into any great details about the many other interesting experiences of discipline, I'll just say his experience or idea of discipline at that time would be the equivalent to what today's society would build a prison on top of him for and name it after him.

My mother had some very interesting disciplinary reactions, also. She might hit you with anything she had in her hand by throwing it at you if you caught her at the wrong time. Or she would send you outside to get a switch. You had to pick it from the hedge bush in front of the house and peel the leaves off of it yourself. It better be long enough and skinny enough to leave welts on your body where it hits you. These are the types of things along with the neighborhood scenes that I described that I've seen as a child that always made me want to run away. *People shouldn't live like this*, I thought. Sometimes, she would use a little paddle that she would send you to the corner store to buy. You know, the ones with the rubber ball attached to a rubber band? She would rip the ball off of the paddle and use that paddle to tan your backside. With all that said, we never felt like we were abused children, and most of the beatings, spankings, whippings, and discipline that we did get was well-deserved.

The norms at that time in society were quite different to what they are now. I had an art teacher in elementary school named Mr. Terrence. He had a thirty-six-inch yard stick that had a ball of duct tape wrapped around the end to make it hard. He would hit us with it for any reason, at any time that he decided we needed discipline. This was acceptable in those times. I wasn't really a bad kid. That type of discipline didn't stop me from doing the things I wanted to do, and it just made me more determined not to get caught. My brother, Craig, on the other hand, became more violent and aggressive.

When my brother joined the Marines, I learned that his tough guy reputation in the neighborhood had been protecting me from all of the other kids. Everybody was afraid of him, and they respected him. Once he joined the Marines, they came at me from all directions. I did not have his protection any longer. Being a very small person, five-feet-six-inches tall, and weighing less than one hundred pounds at seventeen years old, I had learned to exhibit some very violent and interesting behaviors myself. I developed quite a reputation. Some people would warn others to "be careful, he's crazy" because my reaction to any threat could be extreme and very violent.

Craig was a victim of violence and was murdered at twenty-three years old. This was a life-changing event that made me angry and very hard. I walked around carrying a nickel-plated 357 revolver that I had gotten from my Uncle Perry and a little 25 automatic (also from Uncle Perry), looking for trouble and searching for the people responsible for my brother's murder. I did a lot of things to a lot of people, and on quite a few occasions was surprised that I walked away from situations to tell the stories. I once thought I'd murdered a man for nothing. Not really nothing, but because he had pulled a weapon on me the day before and didn't use it. When I caught him by himself with my pistol in his face, he broke down and wept like a little baby. For that, I got angry, stepped back, and pulled the trigger. I saw him put his hands up to his head and fall. I thought I had killed him in broad daylight in front of witnesses. I jumped into my car and drove off.

I later found out that I hadn't killed him and that one of the neighborhood thugs had put a word out that nobody better talk about what had happened or what they saw that day or they would have to face the consequences of his violence. These were my friends. They looked out for me. My view of me around that time in my life was quite different from God's view of me. I saw myself as violent and hard. My actions were indicative of that. I carried two guns and lived a double life. Some people saw me as protecting the good and others saw me as an enforcer. God knew the plans that He had for me and how each experience would more prepare me for His purposes.

On another occasion, in the middle of the night when I was on my way to deliver a package (drugs) to one of my customers, I caught two individuals on my front porch trying to break into my home, which would have been while I was there sleeping. It was almost two or three in the morning. They ran away and hid from the doorway as I was opening the inside door. I got in my car and drove around to look for them. Of course, still planning on delivering my package. Just as I was about to pass by the front door, there they were standing on either side of the street. They opened up on me right in front of my house. I ended up with bullet holes through both my driver and passenger doors and lodged in the back of my swivel back captain's chair in my 1976 Chevy Monte Carlo. Thank God for the steel plates inside the captain's chair. The indentations from the 9-millimeter slugs showed that I would have been shot twice in the back, and the two holes going through my driver's door and into my passenger door showed the track or line of fire as being inches in front of my body. As I drove the car away, four shots would have killed me that day. Just another time that God was watching out for me. Those two guys ended up dead a few weeks later on Linden Boulevard. The word on the street around the neighborhood was that I either did it or arranged it. Though it wasn't me, my reputation grew, and I let it.

There were so many different times when I wondered why I made it. With all of the things that I've been involved in, the situations and circumstances that I came through, I'm not locked up in jail, nor have I ever been. I'm not crippled or dead, and I manage to have what seems to be a reasonable amount of sanity. I used to come home and tell Sandra, my girlfriend at that time, "There's a committee out there somewhere sitting around a table trying to decide ways to destroy or kill me, and they keep failing." I would walk into situations that I walked away from surprised that I walked away. Now, I clearly understand God kept saving me.

One day while visiting my mom in New York, I had an encounter with the police. I'm sure that they picked me as a target and that I was about to die that evening. As I walked from the corner store toward the house on the sidewalk, just at the entrance to the front gate of the yard an unmarked police car with limo-tinted windows pulled up beside me in the street. The front and rear passenger side windows opened. I saw four white men I immediately recognized as plainclothes police.

The one in the back seat asked, "Where are you going?"

I froze and responded, "I'm visiting my mom right here. That's my car beside you."

The man then asked, "What's that in your pocket?"

I knew at that moment that if I had moved wrong that I was going to be shot. I didn't move, but answered slowly and clearly, "That's my Jaguar with the Maryland tags and I am visiting my mom who lives right here." They looked at the car. I'm sure that they noticed the masonic emblems and the SCUBA special tags on the car. They had a short conversation amongst themselves, the windows went up, and they drove off. I'm 100 percent positive that I was about to be a statistic that evening, and the story was going to be four police making a routine stop and the person (me) pulled out a weapon. That's why he was shot.

I'll leave most of those stories for my biography, but here, we're going to talk about some of the epiphanies and encounters with God that caused me to reach a point where I could say that I could see why these things happened. And who was in control? Hmm? I could see the difference between who God saw and who I and the world saw at that time in my life.

So, this was the picture that I saw as a small child born September 10, 1958. A child of the sixties and seventies. A very turbulent time in the history of our country, especially for an African American child. Drugs and violence were prevalent and normal on the streets. At the same time, children and older folks were usually relatively safe in my neighborhood. My family consisted of three different households side by side. I was the middle child of three. My brother, Craig, was a year and a half older. My sister, Beverly, was six years younger. And the next house? That was my grandmother, Aunt Marjorie, my cousin Lucy, my cousin Little Perry, and my Uncle Perry when he wasn't in jail.

As I said earlier, we lived a pretty decent life. My dad was able to and wanted to show us different things and take us to different places to expose us to life from many different angles. I have been taken on trips to Canada, Barbados, and up and down the East Coast to various cities and states. I guess you could say I saw a lot of life by the time I was twenty. I was put into every type of class for activities by the time I was seventeen. I always sucked up knowledge like a sponge. I used to like to read encyclopedias and the dictionary. Before I started college, I had a subscription to *Psychology Today* magazine. Everything mechanical that was given to me, I would immediately take it apart to figure out how it worked and to see if I could put it back together. This always got me in a lot of trouble at the same time. By the time I was twenty, I was able to take two junked Ford Mustangs, a 67 and a 68, buy them for $50 each, strip them down, and build my own one good functioning car, which I drove and maintained for almost four years.

Hindsight being 20/20 vision looking back on me, I realized at some point that I always knew, thought, and had an attitude that I could succeed and do anything I set my mind to. I never imagined, even once, saying I couldn't. So, I experimented with everything and anything. I played all types of games and became pretty good at some: chess, checkers, backgammon, baseball, basketball, football, handball, judo, karate, ballet, and boxing. Any one of those things where there was the slightest bit of pain or discomfort inflicted on me, like the contact sports, I rapidly got rid of.

Wherever there was a need or desire, I would find a way to succeed or accomplish it somehow. Somewhere along the line, I developed a mantra. I used to say, "I've done so much with so little for so long that I'm now qualified to do everything with absolutely nothing." I don't remember where I heard that, but it worked for me.

Around this time in my life, things changed drastically. I saw an ugly picture of the world and most of the people in it. I had no intentions of following any of them or it. I made my own decisions and needed to take charge, be the leader of the pack.

It started when my brother was murdered in a very violent way, which sent me down a path that no one can understand. He was shot multiple times in the face, chest and back and left to die on the sidewalk at Linden Boulevard and 160th Street. My sister and I were just coming home from skating, sometime around midnight, and we had to walk from Jamaica Avenue through the 40 Projects because we had spent all of our bus fare at the roller skating rink. We were probably about two or three blocks from home when a friend jumped out of a car on 160th Street and met us with, "Your brother, Craig, just got shot up on Linden Boulevard. I think you better go up there." I looked at my sister because I knew that he was dead, and I said, "He's gone." I had been telling Craig for a long time that because of his choices and his behaviors that one day he was going to run into somebody just a little bit crazier than me and that they were going to kill him. And that is just what happened. This sent me on a rampage of self-destructive behavior and caused me to start to question and pray those "God, if You really do exist…" type of prayers.

I hope that you are still keeping in mind subliminally the verse that I reminded you to keep there (Romans 8:28) because as you read on, I'm sure that this will all come together for you.

# Chapter 2

I had some interesting epiphanies and experiences in life for the next few years. Once, I was sleeping in the basement where Craig used to sleep. There was very little light and no light sources except for the two small ground level basement windows that allowed just a little bit of moonlight to shine in on the walls of the room. Otherwise, it was pitch black. I was praying and I remember saying to God, "If You really do exist, I just want an opportunity to talk to my brother one more time to tell him that I do love him." I felt bad about the way I treated him because I realized he was always trying to get closer to me and that he looked up to me, but I looked down on him because of his mistakes and his ways.

This particular night as I lay there praying, at the foot of my bed sat a silhouette of Craig as clear as day. I should say a hologram. A black hologram in a pitch-black room. Darker than the darkness that was there. If you remember in my description of myself, I was the one who always needed to understand and study everything so it made sense. This made no sense to me. There could not be a shadow where there was no light source. There was no similar item or shape in the room to block any light sources or create shadow. So, I lay there trying to make sense of what source caused the light or the shadow to sit like a hologram on the corner of the bed, a three-dimensional figure darker than the darkness in the room. I never did come to any conclusions about the source of light because the light that shone through the window was so minimal and the line of direction was nowhere near the silhouette in the room.

I concluded that this dark shadow or silhouette or hologram was a spirit. Even though I thought I was an atheist, I had always known that there was something supernatural far beyond our understanding that we just don't comprehend yet. The existence of spirits wasn't far from my belief. Nevertheless, I accepted that Craig's spirit was sitting there, so I had the discussion with him that I wanted to have. I never saw that spirit, shadow or silhouette again, but I was comfortable with telling him that I did love him. While he was there, I did get an opportunity to apologize for not expressing or allowing him the opportunity to express his love toward me. I never took it into consideration. This might have been God answering my prayers, saying, "I am here, and I'm about to prepare you for the plans I have for you."

One of the self-destructive habits that I had developed around that time while searching for a resolve and the answers to my brother's murder was walking the streets of South Jamaica, especially through the projects and around my neighborhood at all hours of the night. I would often roam and find myself sitting back on my mother's front porch at two or three in the morning. One night while sitting on the step, I noticed a girl in beautiful white dress coming out of the projects at 110th Avenue and 159th Street in the direction to walk through my mother's block. As she got closer and closer, I realized she was the most beautiful young woman that I could ever imagine or remember imagining and seeing. She was just peacefully strolling along as if floating down the street. Maybe 20 feet or so out from the stoop where I sat is where her path crossed in front of me. The first time I saw her, it had to be around two in the morning. I watched her in amazement, thinking to myself, *This poor lady does not know the danger that she's in.* The *streets that she walks.* The same danger that I was out there looking for as an escape or an outlet for my anger. She was just strolling through it as if it didn't exist. I thought to myself, *I hope nothing happens to her,* because I knew all of the possibilities. It didn't seem that she had any idea that there was anybody within eyesight. Even noticing her existence, I never spoke that night. Neither did she.

On another night, within the next week or so, I was in the same position, sitting on my mother's stoop some time around two in the morning, and here comes that wonderful vision again out of 40 Projects floating up the street. While I watched her come closer and closer, I realized again the dangers that she was facing. The same dangers I was out there looking to encounter. Something in my spirit touched me and pushed me to protect her. To help her and to let her know how ignorant she was of the dangers that she faced. I spoke, I walked out into the street, and I walked with her to the end of the block, which wasn't very far.

I talked with her about the violence that she could possibly encounter and that if I was one of those people who might do her harm, she would have been a prime target for me. Her reply was so peaceful, so humble, so quiet. She listened intently, smiled at me, and said, "I'm not alone." I remember thinking to myself, *This child is crazy.* So, I went on to try to educate her and prove to her the dangers that she faced. Her reply was still the same in a very quiet and calm, peaceful voice with a smile on her face, which brought peace to me. I didn't know yet that our spirits had connected nevertheless because of her peace. I left her and went back to sitting on the stoop.

I left her because she was walking toward Baisley projects where I was sure that, if I should get caught alone in that area, especially in the middle of the night by myself, that friends of the people who killed my brother would notice me and certainly see that I did not make it out of there alive. Not that I was concerned about dying, but I was more concerned about dying before I got my opportunity to get revenge on the people who murdered my brother. So, I went back to the stoop, satisfied with the fact that I thought I had given a good effort to educate the young lady, give her wise advice, and walk her past the most dangerous area of her walk. That was the second encounter.

There was a third and final encounter. Maybe a week or so later. I was on the stoop again around the same time in the middle of the night. A time that no decent person should be walking the streets of South Jamaica, Queens, especially someone as beautiful as her in a floating white dress looking like an angel, yet here she came floating down the street again. This time, I decided to protect her. I was not going to allow her to be attacked because the odds were really against her after repeating the same dangerous behaviors and choices that, one day, she wasn't going to make it to her destination. So this particular day, I walked with her. I had the same conversation and she replied with the same peace and assurance that she was not alone, and she was sure that she was safe and there was no need for me to worry. I did not believe her, but I did come to understand that this was faith. It was her faith. She did tell me about her relationship with Jesus the Christ. She did tell me about where she came from and where she was going. She was coming from an Apostolic church service that often let out late in the night, and her faith allowed her to be confident that she would always be safe and that no danger would befall her that wasn't God's will.

Looking back, I know this to be a seed of faith that God planted in my spirit. Another step in the process of drawing me to a right relationship with Him and helping me to understand something that I might not come to see for decades. I never saw her again. She often crosses my mind, and I do know the faith that she spoke of. There were many other interesting happenings that I experienced over the next ten years or so. Some of them touched on the questions of spirituality and God's existence. Others were the far end of the spectrum and involved street violence, criminal activity, and self-destructive behavior. They ranged from one end of the spectrum to the other and everything in between. Too many to mention or go into any detail about. Those two encounters, the spirit of my brother on the bed and the young lady who I believed to have been an angel in the street, were the most powerful and significant.

My life was so convoluted around this time. I still managed to fool the world somewhat and had a double life going on: fighting with my demons and searching for resolutions. I was probably sniffing four to five grams of cocaine a day along with drinking at least about a fifth bottle of scotch. I used to jokingly say, "I've sniffed Peru," all while managing and operating the welding business and the photo processing lab. On top of the fact that I was a cocaine dealer, which supported my unbeknownst to me habit, it also kept me running day and night.

Something happened that caused me to pause and take a good look at my life. I ran out of money; not so much out of money, but I went to pay my bills and it was time to re-up (buy more cocaine supply). I didn't have enough money for both. I was so used to having a comfortable cash flow that I never really kept records or track. I assessed my situation and realized that I was sniffing too much cocaine. The simple solution was to stop. That's when I realized a bigger issue: I was an addict.

The concept of being a cocaine addict was unacceptable. I thought I was in control of my world and everything going on in it and around me. The concept of anything controlling my life was not only unacceptable, but extremely frightening. I went to my mom's house and had a discussion with my parents. They both suggested that I go into a rehab center. Another unacceptable concept. It took me almost a year before I could say that I successfully managed to ween myself from the cocaine habit by cutting back a little at a time. It was difficult, but I succeeded. All things working; God had a plan!

For many years since I was a teenager, I used to tell my mom that the first chance I got, I was out of there. People were not supposed to live like this, and I knew that if I stayed in New York, especially after what happened to my brother, my behavior, experiences, choices, and the signals I seemed to be receiving that I would either be dead or in jail very soon, neither of which is what I intended for myself. I said that to her so much. She told me she was tired of hearing it and wished I would go ahead and do it.

Without going into a great deal of explanation as to how I came to meet a gentleman from Kansas City and took his word on the job that I would have once I moved there, that is exactly what happened. I met a girl on a cruise who lived in Kansas City. A friend of her family, who was also on the cruise, worked in the construction industry. After I told him about my life in New York and how I had always wanted to move, he said if I could document all of the experience that I had in my welding business and my skill levels that he would promise me an opportunity to start my life over in a better place with a good job. So, I packed my stuff, I traded in my Cadillac Cimarron for a beat up old Dodge van, put my welding machine, some tools, my clothes, and my computer in the van, and hopped on the road with Billy Kay (the lady I met).

In Kansas City, I fell into the same behaviors and patterns that I had in New York. I loved the clubs. I loved the nightlife. I loved the music. I hung out. I found the worst places to hang out, but to me, they weren't bad. They were normal and what I was comfortable with was the atmosphere. I was familiar with it. Drugs and violence were all around me.

This leads me to the third and most powerful explanation of God's way of banging me over the head, saying, "I'm trying to get your attention, so pay attention!" The sign at the corner of the Alameda. It may have been the Paseo in Kansas City, Missouri, where I was staying at the time with Billy Kay. She would often invite me to go to Bible studies with her. I usually refused, knowing my tendency to challenge the Bible at every turn and remembering how much I enjoyed allowing the Jehovah's Witnesses into my mother's home. When my mom and parents would hide in the kitchen and say don't answer the door when they saw them coming, I would gladly let them in and sit on the couch and talk with them for hours, challenging their claims and teachings.

Little did I know that it was God. He was teaching me the stories in the Bible and the things that would prepare me for the future. Planting seeds that had plenty of time to develop strong roots. I took her up on one of those offers to go to Bible study. She brought me a Bible, a King James Version. How much fun was that starting off reading a King James Version of the Bible with its Old English writings? That first Bible study was very challenging, but involved. It was an interactive Bible study, and the people leading the Bible study were intrigued and enjoyed the challenge, the discussion, and the involvement to the point of inviting and extending requests inviting me back. That was to my amazement. Hindsight is 20/20 vision. Now, I realize just more seeds that God was planting.

As I said, I really love jazz music, the clubs, the nightlife, and the bars that had no fear of traveling and going to strange places by myself. I recognized the dangers all around me. They were almost like my comfort zone, and the people who would be considered dangerous factors usually were the people who embraced me. People usually respect the same things and tools that they try to use against others, so they knew I spoke their language. I felt like I was one of them. Not just one of them, but maybe the leader. I used to be met with greetings like, "Hey, what's up, New York?" New York became a nickname in a lot of different places.

One night, I must have left my lights on in my van because my battery went dead at a club that I was hanging out in. So, I had to call Billy Kay and tell her where I was and ask her to come meet me or give me a boost. When I told her the club that I was at, she went into a panic and cried. She had so much fear that she called her relatives and family all that she could gather up and they all came out to get me to save me from the dangerous crowd that they thought I was in the middle of trouble and in danger. They thought I was surrounded and in trouble only to find me there, the leader of the pack with all of the thugs in the neighborhood, laughing and joking and having a good time. I didn't understand that fear as they told me stories about how many people had gotten shot up there. That didn't faze me in the least little bit. I just learned not to let them know that that's where I was going.

Oftentimes, I would go out and have too much to drink and get lost and try to find my way back to where I lived. Just like in New York, I was perfectly fine with being lost. Each time I got lost, I just found a new way. Learned new things. Most of the time when I got lost in Kansas City, I would come upon this particular intersection. I believe it was the Paseo and the Alameda (definitely one of those two streets). That something is not important right now. What's important is the sign. There was a big black sign, one of the biggest billboards you could see, maybe twenty by forty feet. It was solid black, but in the center in small print, it said, "All you have to do is ask."

That sign was my landmark. I knew that if I made a left at that intersection, I knew my way home from there. So, at least three or four times that I can remember coming to that side and being relieved, thinking, *Ah. Now I know my way home.* Remember, God works in all things. One night, I came to that sign at that same intersection just as lost as before. I stopped at the corner at a red light, looked at that sign, and for the first time, I wondered, *What does that mean?* At that moment, my van cut off. It just stopped running. Hmm. Now, what? Okay, I was out of gas. So weird to get right there and run out of gas. Luckily for me, I had my welding machine in the back which had a small two-gallon gas tank on it. And it had gas in it. I figured I would just syphon the gas out of the welders tank into my van tank and make it home. That was when I noticed that at the bottom of the sign in the far right corner was a scripture verse.

To this day, I don't remember, nor have I tried to research what scripture verse it was. I do remember that at that time, I looked it up in the Bible that Billy Kay had given me. It was a scripture verse leading me to the acceptance of Jesus Christ for salvation of my soul. Before I left that corner and got my van running, I prayed another prayer. "Okay, God. I see that You do exist. I see You hear my prayers. I recognize that you're banging me over the head and trying to get my attention and send me a message. That You do exist and that all I need to do is open up my heart." There that night, I prayed. I guess that would be what most churches call the prayer of salvation. I accepted that God did exist and had been working with me and that He was trying to draw me to a relationship with Him. Because of my unfamiliarity with the Old and New Testament and the doctrine of salvation through Jesus Christ, I was just simply settled in on the idea that God does exist and was calling me. I heeded the call.

I'd like to take a moment to take you to another scripture verse that I know and have come to know as one of the most powerful verses in my Christian walk. Jesus said, *No man can come to me, except the Father which hath sent me draws him* (John 6:44 KJV). Well, that sign there in Kansas City, Missouri. What's the third epiphany? He said to me, "I'm drawing you," and it was the moment I received and accepted redemption and salvation. So, it didn't change my character and behavior as much as it changed my perspective and my belief. I was still the same person. God had made me with the same characteristics, the same habits. The only difference was I had a Bible and a very strong urge to take that thing apart to either prove it to be right or prove it to be wrong, but I was going to know one way or the other.

Shortly after that, I came to realize that Kansas City, Missouri was not the place for me. I could not be upwardly mobile there, and I was no longer feeling in my spirit that I was where I belonged. One day, while nobody was around, I packed my stuff, jumped in my van, and ran away from home. I headed back to New York to start over again, but my determination to leave New York never changed. I was only there again for a short time, saving some dollars and preparing for the next attempt at starting over.

One time, I was on a trip to DC with my friend Maxine. It was the middle of the crack epidemic, and I was making money putting steel bars on everybody's windows to keep crackheads from climbing in and out. I decided that somewhere between DC and Baltimore was an excellent place to start my business, putting steel bars on people's windows and homes because I could cover the demand in both cities. So, I found an apartment, a sight unseen in Columbia, Maryland.

By this time, I was taking that Bible apart, reading it often, and listening to a lot of gospel music all the time while still hanging out in bars and the jazz clubs. The only difference was now, I spent a lot of time when I wasn't partying and drinking working really hard reading that Bible and listening to gospel music. My friends would ask, "Why are you always listening to that gospel music?" My answer was always that I liked it, but I was really feeding my spirit and it was watering my soul. It helped me to develop roots, roots that had been nurturing and growing in my soul since I was a small child challenging the Jehovah's Witnesses in my mother's living room.

I had no idea how much knowledge God had already instilled in me about the Bible. I started feeling driven to go to different Bible studies. I would walk into any church where I saw a sign that said Bible study. If it had a date and time, I would just walk in and sit in the corner. I did this for almost two years. I just sat in on people's Bible studies. I found the Bible studies to be interesting and educational, especially the interactive ones. The interactive ones were usually the ones that would cause me to attend the church service on Sundays, and as always, not participate. In most cases, the people were overly welcoming and eager to have new visitors and members come in. In some cases, I was not very welcome because oftentimes on Sunday morning I would come into the church smelling like scotch or vodka that I had drunk the night before, which I wasn't ashamed of. I felt like the church was supposed to accept me as I was and if I wasn't welcome, I didn't belong there. There were quite a few that made me feel unwelcome. Soon, I'll write my biography and it will have details of many stories that go in between the spaces and questions that are left unanswered here, but for now, let's move on to my ministry, or the ministry that God did through me, and by using me.

## Nugget

I've heard it said that right and wrong is a consensus of opinion. This would mean that if everybody tells you that something is a certain way or there's something that either exists or it doesn't, the majority of the people, if they are in agreement, decide what's true, false, right, or wrong. On the subject of spirituality or whether or not there is a God and looking at that theory, you must concede that mankind has proven there must be a God. That there is a higher power, a spiritual existence that we can't pinpoint, or all agree on at the same time.

The proof of this is that since the beginning of time, since we can find pictures and depictions carved and scratched on cave walls long before we have historical writings, there's evidence that all of mankind, every civilization that has developed any form of communication, has always attempted to develop a relationship with a higher power. Worshipping some type of God and nurturing a relationship with some type of spiritual higher power. So, if every form of civilization has fostered and attempted to develop these relationships, then it stands to reason that the consensus of opinion is there is a God, a higher power. Regardless of what you call Him or how you perceive Him (or her) and your religious beliefs, they really don't matter. We all strive for that higher level of spirituality. We are first spiritual beings experiencing a physical existence which is a preparation for that higher level of existence. A spiritual existence that we look forward to. God is real.

Since I've come to accept the fact that there is a God in my studies, I've come to realize that I am not very religious, but I am very spiritual. Looking at the Bible, I see that Jesus was the same way. He didn't have a problem until He went to church. You see Him repeatedly challenging and teaching the leaders in the synagogues of the church and society, the Sadducees, the Pharisees, and the Sanhedrin. *They worship me in vain; their teachings are merely human rules* (Matt. 15:9 NIV).

# Chapter 3

**The call and the church. What God did through my ministry within the AME church and Called and Chosen Ministries.**

It was around the late 1990s, during a period of transition from Kansas City back to New York and Maryland. All the while systematically studying, listening to gospel music, and taking that King James Bible apart, behind the scenes being watered by the Word. Again, I did not see a change that was happening within me. I had a job at G. Krug and Son. They used to have Bible studies on Wednesday mornings. Most of the employees didn't join in, mainly just the upper management and the office workers. Occasionally, I would join in, sit down, and listen to the study, the prayer, and the Word. I was always impressed by Warren one of the managers, as he led in prayer. His prayers seemed so heartfelt from deep within his soul. If I could, I wanted to pray like that. By this time, I had accepted that God was real, but I didn't completely realize what He was doing within me. Still, somewhere along that line, I was trying to disprove and challenge the Bible, and my curiosity was to be fulfilled.

Jumping off of the subject for a moment, I remember once when I was in my college years, I had a dream. I dreamed of myself speaking in front of large crowds of people. I remembered dismissing that dream as some type of delusion of grandeur. Hindsight is 20/20 vision. Looking back on that dream or vision, I realized that it was a vision. It was God giving me a glimpse of my future as a minister in the church.

Moving forward to the late 1990s at G. Krug and Son, I was still challenging the teachings of the Bible, but not the existence of a higher power. Anthony, a painter at the shop at the time, came running into the office excitedly and said, "Mr. Johnson! Mr. Johnson! I had a dream last night. That you were in a church in a pulpit and preaching!" I thought it was the funniest vision or dream, not remembering the vision that God had given me almost twenty years earlier.

Steve, the owner of the company at that time, was sitting at his desk and heard the conversation. I looked at Steve with a puzzled look on my face and said, "Could you picture that? Me, in a church, preaching?"

Steve sat back in his chair, also with a puzzled look. He pondered the idea for a moment, then he looked at me with a very serious face and said, "I can see that."

My response to that I remember specifically. I said out loud, "Both of you are crazier than lunatics." I laughed it off and went back to work.

This brings me to the next ten years in ministry. It was around that time I used to stop in on Bible studies. At any sign that I may have passed, I would just walk in and sit down and listen. I did this at many different churches and many different places all over the state of Maryland. I went quite often, sometimes even places where they did not speak English. Usually somebody would translate. Most of the time, I was welcome. Very rarely did I speak. I just listened and observed. It didn't seem strange to me. It always felt like I belonged wherever I was. And when it didn't, something in my spirit would tell me to leave, which I was never hesitant to do, regardless of what was going on or being said at the time.

One Sunday, I heard Pastor Anne Fuller preach. It was streaming on the radio. She was so charismatic, and the sermon was so powerful. The message was so real and fitting for me. I felt so drawn in my spirit and felt I had to be there. I had to go and hear more of this dynamic preacher's messages and teachings. I had to find Mt. Calvary AME.

I found that church and visited one Sunday morning, not knowing anything about AME church etiquette. I walked in and sat on one of the front pews, and there I sat and listened to the sermon. I felt the atmosphere and felt the spirit of the Lord there. I felt like I belonged there. Nobody disturbed me, even though I was sitting in the wrong seat. I was sitting in a row with administrators and the leaders of the church, but nobody told me that I was out of order.

They had a Saturday morning Bible study there. Sister Willette was the leader. She was also a dynamic teacher and filled with the spirit. I enjoyed her Bible studies even more than I enjoyed the sermons and Sunday mornings. So, I made it a practice to show up for Bible study on Saturday morning almost every Saturday, regardless of the fact that the smell of the scotch or vodka that I had been drinking the night before was so strong and pungent on me that everyone in the room was probably offended by my presence. I usually sat in the corner quietly and didn't speak very much, but I learned.

The Bible studies became regular. That was where I went on Saturday morning, regardless of my condition or what time I had gotten in the night before. Something else was happening around the same time. I could hang out at a bar until two in the morning, drive home staggering drunk, fall asleep, and wake up at 4:44 a.m.

The reason I'm being specific about this is because it happened regularly and quite often, I would wake up, look at the clock, it would be exactly 4:44. Also, I'd be as straight as an arrow. The smell from the vodka or alcohol, whatever I had been drinking was usually still with me, but the effects were gone. I was wide awake, clear-minded, and would sit and study and read the Word, still trying to disprove it somewhere in my mind. As opposed to realizing that God was getting into me, my habit was to always take on the characters I was reading about. I put myself in their place.

One story in particular was Simon Peter's story. I had never heard the teachings of Simon Peter or that he was a coward, so I did not perceive him with any preconceived opinions. I saw him as Jesus saw him. I won't give you a detailed explanation, but Jesus turns Simon Peter into a spy. Simon Peter had no choice but to do what Jesus had predicted, but for now, I'll continue with what God was doing. It was one day in Bible study the question was asked, "Who was Simon Peter?" Many of the attendants in the class started responding with, "He was a coward," "He was the one who denied Jesus," or "He was the one who didn't fulfill his responsibility." Everybody had something negative to say about Simon Peter except myself, and for the first time, I joined in on the conversation. "Peter was not a coward," I explained. "Simon Peter was there, making sure that he was as close to Jesus as he could be through the whole process. My question is, where were the other disciples?" This was one of the first times I joined in on the conversation. It was a very lively conversation. Everybody seemed to enjoy it and get a lot out of it.

From that point on, every Saturday morning began to be like that. The class started to grow. Attendance increased. There was murmuring and talks throughout the church that I knew nothing about, but they talked about the young man who comes into the Bible study and initiates these wonderful interactive conversations.

Who knew what God was doing? Anyway, moving right along on another occasion, Sister Willette had some family business in Florida she had to attend to. She reached out to me and asked if I would lead her class next Saturday morning because of how much she enjoyed the way that I prompted much of the interactive discussions and studies that we were now enjoying. My answer was, "Let me pray about it and see how it feels in my spirit." This soon became my answer to everything.

I'm sure by now you know where this is going. I led quite a few Bible studies and became quite involved in the Saturday classes. I went to quite a few more services and eventually became a regular in the church. I don't think anybody knew back then that I wasn't even a member. This went on for some time. They gave me a title in the Christian education department, and they allowed me to lead some of the adult Bible studies in the sanctuary or on Saturday mornings. Sometimes, even the pastor was there and always looked at me with amazement.

My new friend Donnie told me something I knew nothing about. We used to talk about my past and my life and where I currently was. She was a psychologist and a very good one. So, one day she told me I was a teacher. That's what I was, and that's what I had always been. I looked at myself from a different perspective and realized she was right. I had been doing that with everyone that I encountered my whole life. Then she told me that I was an enigma. I didn't know what an enigma was or what that meant. Once she explained it to me, I realized, again, that she was right. I did not fit in. I was very unusual. A single straight Black man who ventured into the church without any connections or restrictions and embraced everybody and was embraced by everybody. Just like one of those Sesame Street teachings where they say, "Which of these things just doesn't belong?" I didn't really fit, but at the same time, I fit perfectly.

By the time that I actually joined the church, the pastor walked up to me, hugged me, and whispered quietly in my ear, "I've been waiting for you." I realized that she was the only one who knew. Over time, I became more and more involved. Somebody would come to me and say they wanted me to lead a ministry. I would say, "Let me pray about it. Let me see how it feels in my spirit." Usually, everything that I was asked, I felt in my spirit that God wanted me to do. The finance ministry, the Christian education department, the new members of ministry, when the pastor asked me to be on her board. I asked her if she knew who I was She said, "Yes. I have a group of board members who would agree with everything I say simply because I said it. But you will be the one who will challenge me. Every good leader needs somebody who's not afraid to tell them when their stuff stinks." I was impressed and accepted that role.

Soon after that, she came to me, sat me down, and said, "I want you to be a part of my new member's class." Well, I prayed about it, and of course, the Lord led me to accept. It wasn't long after that she came to me and told me, "I set a date for you. You will preach your trial sermon." Wow, look at God. Remember that vision? I think the membership at that time may have been a few thousand members, not to mention the fact that the service was televised and broadcasted nationally. Two Visions: The first being Anthony's dream, and the other, me twenty years later, having a vision of speaking in front of a large crowd of people.

How could I question anymore that God was purposely orchestrating His plan? That He had been orchestrating all along? That was actually where He wanted me to be, whether I liked it or not because from my perspective, I was being dragged into a situation kicking and screaming, "No, no, I don't want to go! Don't make me go!" Imagine a child being pulled into a room going into an operation or procedure they're definitely afraid of, holding on to the edges of the door with both hands and feet, screaming and crying, "Don't make me do it! No, Mommy, save me! No, Daddy, don't make me go! Don't make me do it!"

This was how I felt in my flesh, but in my spirit, I knew this was where I was supposed to be. It certainly was not where I wanted to be because God certainly challenged me at every turn in these situations. I would find myself the only person in the room without stripes on my sleeve or initials before and after my name. I would look at myself insignificantly fitting into this room with the likes of Bishop Vashti McKenzie, Pastor Frank Reid, and many of the other major leaders, movers, and shakers in the AME church at the time were people from all over the world and all over the country. There I sat, still in the corner, quietly trying not to say what God put into my spirit and finding it bursting out of me many times.

Oftentimes, I would find myself looking up at the sky, saying to God, "This is not funny." In almost all of my Christian education classes, I purposely avoided the subject of tithing. The spiritual concept was not being followed biblically, as far as I was concerned, according to the AME way. So, I knew that it was a sore spot that I should not touch on. Applying any wisdom would create a problem. One day, we were having a special conference. One of the bishops from Africa, Bishop Vashti Mackenzie from the United States, and many other leaders from the AME church all over the country where there sitting in the pulpit. I walked into the 7:00 a.m. service only to find Pastor Fuller standing there at the door waiting for me. Happy to see me, she said, "Brother Darrel, I need you to fill in ten minutes in the service. I want you to speak on tithing." Wow.

I looked straight up through the ceiling into the heavens and said, "God, this is now funny," knowing what was coming.

I did give a biblically correct ten- or fifteen-minute teaching on tithing from a spiritual perspective that nobody could challenge or stop me in the middle of for being wrong, but at the same time, what came out of me was not in keeping with the AME way and certainly gave the impression that the leadership of the church was wrong. If you can imagine the feeling of fifteen or twenty very powerful people standing behind you with the ability to shoot fire out of their eyes, this was my experience. I stood there speaking and in the middle of saying, "The least you could do is tithe." I didn't consider myself a tither because I didn't bother to count. I gave according to how my spirit guided me and according to how blessed I was. Nevertheless, however it came out (I'm sure there's a recording nobody could challenge), I saw the whole congregation in front of me with an expression of "oh" on their faces. At the same time, everybody's head seemed to cock slightly to the left. Who could believe that? The things that I was saying as a leader of the AME church standing in front of all of the other leadership. I saw all of the faces in front of me, and I felt the fire and the anger of all of the leadership standing behind me. It was almost as if I was in front of a firing squad. I finished, sat down, and prayed.

Almost a month had passed after that before Pastor Fuller finally pulled me into her office to tell me that I could not say the things that I said in front of the congregation in an AME church. I reiterated to her that what I said was biblical and that everything I taught was correct. She was over her anger, but by then, I guess somewhere the leadership realized that we could not make that mistake again. I was assigned to pulpit duty at both services every Sunday morning for the next year, but I was not allowed to speak, nor was I allowed to do the benediction. To read the

Scripture, to introduce the Word, to pray the invocation. I was just allowed to sit there quietly. People who watched the services on cable TV reached out to me on a few occasions to ask me why I wasn't allowed to do anything anymore. My answer was always, "I'm sanctified." When asked what I meant by that, the answer was always, "I'm set aside for a special purpose."

I did come to realize that God had placed me in that situation. Even some of the leaders in the AME church said and referred to the AME way as a demonic process. God placed me there so I could learn, understand, and be in a position to make change from within. Also, so I could learn patience. That I could learn to love the sometimes unlovable. That I could learn to forgive. And could give God full control of every situation and circumstance, regardless of how it appeared to me at the time.

Thinking of the amazing things that God did while I was at Mt. Calvary AME, it reminds me of a time when the leadership of Mt. Calvary went to what we called a silent retreat. It was at Our Lady of Mount Provenance Convent where the Oblate Sisters of Providence hosted us. Who would have ever imagined me in a convent, much less me in a convent for two or three days in complete silence surrounded by nuns.

Early one morning while I was at the Oblate Sisters Convent, I decided to take a morning walk in the woods. A perfect opportunity to commune with nature. I came upon a fallen tree, and I sat on it. There I sat, as still as the tree, marveling at God's creation in total silence and peace. I didn't hear the deer approaching, but almost instantly, there was a deer standing within two feet of my face. We were looking eye to eye. Not only was this amazing to me, but my thoughts were it seemed that the deer was just as much at peace as I was. He was not afraid of me, nor was I afraid of him. We both knew that we were safe. The Spirit of the Lord was with us there in the garden. Those few days that I got to spend with myself, with the Spirit of the Lord, and in perfect peace I'll never forget. I recommend a silent retreat to anyone who has never tried one.

There are so many more lessons, experiences, and interesting sets of circumstances that happened through the ministry process that God put me through. You'll have to wait for the biography to hear some of those in detail. We'll see what the Lord does. Moving right along.

By now, I was involved in so many different aspects of leadership in the AME church. It was some time around 2001 when God spoke to me in another epiphany, clearly gave me my call, and told me I was going to lead. There were no more questions or doubts. It was also around that same time, in another epiphany, that God told me to start writing. That I was going to write in my attempts at being obedient, which I was not particularly good at. I started journaling as I read through my journals from back in 2001 (I journaled off and on for about two years). The most significant changes in my ministry were in those first two years. Let me correct that not the most significant changes, but the revelations of God's plan became much clearer at that time.

Soon thereafter, I started dating Reverend Rosemary. At that time, I owned two apartment buildings in Curtis Bay. We started using one of the apartments as a room for Bible studies so my tenants and anyone who wanted to enjoy a Bible study could have a place to come. The AME leadership found out about this and told us we could not do that without it being sanctioned by them. That we must also take collections and bring them to the AME church. This was unacceptable in my vision because everything that I was doing was through the leading of the Holy Spirit and I was not guided to do that. That's when the fight started. I refused and was challenged at every turn and told that I could not do that as a member of the leadership in the AME church. I thought this was quite funny because what were they going to do, fire me from doing God's will? Impossible.

I just went along doing what I felt led to do. It was with an "Okay, so now you're mad. What next?" attitude. Nevertheless, Rosemary and I began Called and Chosen Ministries, which rapidly began to grow. We married and started having services. Everything that we needed God provided. Somebody gave us a location in an old school building to use for our services. Somebody gave us a van to use for transportation. Everything that we needed was always provided. We never had to ask the congregation, never had to prompt or push anyone, or use brainwashing techniques to guilt them into giving. In fact, I never once took a paycheck or any money from the church or the ministry work that I've done out of the churches and services. The leadership of other churches would often write us checks and I always put the check back in the basket to be used for the ministry of that church. Even in our own services, the bills were paid and the responsibilities were taken care of.

Almost every Sunday afternoon, I would take whoever was left of the congregation that was willing to go, and we would all go out to lunch and enjoy fellowship together and represent the example of what God called us to represent in public. Christian soldiers fulfilling God's will. As I was saying quite a few times in the past, the responsibility that God had placed on me was enjoyable and easy because it was spirit led and because whenever my flesh got involved, I really did not want to do it. So much of my picture of many of the ministers that I saw and had the opportunity to get to know disturbed me quite often because of the high level of discernment that God had given me. And so many of the hearts of those I saw involved were not led by spirit or faith, but more ambition and drive; not something that God did, but something that they did or attempted to do with little faith.

Matthew 17:18-20 (NIV) speaks of this. *Then the disciples came to Jesus in private and asked, "Why couldn't we drive it out?" He replied, "Because you have so little faith. Truly I tell you, if you have faith as small as a mustard seed, you can say to this mountain, 'Move from here to there,' and it will move. Nothing will be impossible for you."*

God used me in many ways through and during my ministry at the AME church while teaching and preparing me personally. Then through the union of Rosemary and myself and the development of Called and Chosen Ministries, many good things happened. There was much more personal and spiritual growth along with many lives being changed, touched, and helped. God did some wonderful stuff with it all. This brings us back to, "All Things." Even though that particular union was not part of God's plan, it was part of our plan that we injected into God's plan. God used it well.

I'm feeling the need to give some clarification to the circumstances and facts that are all well documented that led to the dissolvement of my marriage to Rosemary. So, I include it here. The information as I wrote it in a letter to Rosemary, which I called my certificate of divorce. The contents of that letter were as follows:

*Rosemary,*

*The purpose of this letter is to reiterate and clarify my thoughts and position in this matter. Please do not take it as an attack or assault on you, but for information purposes and edification only. It is a Bible study in part. You did say on more than one occasion that you thought that divorce was not biblical, and we disagreed. I will now take the time to show a powerful biblical reference juxtaposing our circumstances and the biblical example. In Jeremiah 3:1-14, God divorced Israel.*

*Without going into great detail on verses 1 through 7, the overview is that God's chosen people had given themselves to chasing after other things of the world; unholy, ungodly. Physical relationships and other religious beliefs. God, through the prophet Jeremiah, told His people to repent and return to Him. They put these things and actions before God. This is idolatry. Any relationship with lustful behavior that puts anything before God is considered adulterous behavior. God held back His blessings. Verse 8 in the New International Version, "I gave faithless Israel her certificate of divorce and sent her away because of her adulteries."*

*In our situation, your motives were never pure, they were based. In you fulfilling your lust after the acquisition of things, the greed for money and the lust for attention, position, and recognition. A bigger house, a fancier car, self-aggrandizing needs to satisfy validation issues, a husband in name, and all at the same time, you were involved in an inappropriate, secretive relationship with that male friend of yours. I didn't hold back any blessings, but attempted to continue to fulfill all of the desires of your heart and be a good and godly husband to you while continuing to honor my vows to God. Your behavior toward me and our relationship is the same type of behavior that caused God to issue a certificate of divorce to His people in verse 8.*

*In versus 9 through 13 (NIV), the word of God reiterates this same behavior and points out that "'Judah did not return to me with all her heart, but only in pretense' declares the Lord." The Word of God then exhibits God's love by presenting opportunity for His undeserving people to return to right their relationship with Him. A way to correct the problem. A solution to the situation. Verse 13, "only acknowledge your guilt."*

*In our situation, you acknowledged only part of your guilt and at the same time, purposefully painted a false picture of me to make me look as if I was the problem. We were in counselling for three and a half* years, thank you. I grew much, and in September 2006, we sat in a session and agreed that we would start over. You promised to work on your ways, but at the same time, you had already instituted your destructive plan and were hiding money for the fulfillment of that plan. Working hard at painting a false, defamatory picture of me and attempting to provoke me into the type of behavior that would solidify your claim. And your plan? This is what the Bible refers to as wicked devices. You didn't bother to alter your behavior in any way. Your words didn't match your actions. This is pretense. Your provocations failed.

The truth always comes to light.

You spent at least a year building your plan and painting that false picture of me that, to your surprise, no one believed. Then you started making false accusations of abusive behavior, which also backfired. And then he resorted to threatening to call the police and make false accusations to, as you put it, prove a point. All of this is documented in my written communications to you and our counselor, Doctor Pride, during this tumultuous time. In case you are deluded, maybe you would refer back to those emails and letters. Your plan failed. Let's call a snake a snake.

You see, as I said above, God was a divorcee. I'm not comparing myself to God, but to the example that He gave me and His word. My situation with you is the same. God divorced Israel and Judah due to their behavior and actions against Him. Wicked devices. This is the same as your unholy, unfaithful, destructive character defaming and downright violent behavior toward me. The conditions that God set forth in verse 13 for Him to accept Israel back with the same as the conditions that you were faced with and refused to do, only acknowledge your guilt. It is now over. Let it be that way.

Darrel Johnson.

With all of that said and clarified, moving right along here. I'm still doing ministry. It's just not confined to the walls of the traditional organized denominational divisions of the church as we know it today. God is still using me to touch lives. He's still growing me and maturing me. And even though at this point in my life we're coming to the end of this book or the end of this story, I, like Paul and Silas, find myself in a set of circumstances that has opened the door up for multi-level miracles. They are happening all around us currently. I'm happy and at peace. It is well with my soul. I am truly blessed.

This leads me into the last few chapters. What's happening right now? The revelations and the diagnosis.

In 2022, I had another epiphany. God began to remind me of the mission that He had given me over twenty years ago and continued reminding me regularly from all different angles and sides. People would come to me and tell me things about what I should be writing. They told me they would like to hear my memoirs and it seemed to come at me from all angles all the time. Almost every discussion I got into, somebody would say, "You should write about that," or "How come you haven't written a book?" It was over and over again.

I kept remembering God had instructed me to start writing over twenty years ago. I collected many of the bits and pieces of information, many of which you have read already in this book. Some of the nuggets and stories I have been collecting and putting them together in little file folders on disk drives and computers or notes. So, within the past year, I started digging through and purging the information. Realizing that God was saying, "Hey. You didn't fulfill the mission I gave you."

Six months passed and I had another epiphany. I started having dreams, but these dreams were more powerful and sometimes frightening. My recently deceased parents were coming to me regularly, sending me messages telling me to come and beckoning me on. I would also have violent dreams about things that should have killed me in the past. I would have visions of experiences that I've had that God had saved me from. All of those things started coming at me from every angle. It was like my life was flashing before me.

Sometime around August of the same year, God spoke to me again in another epiphany. At this time, very clearly, He said, "Your time is near. It's time to complete what I've instructed you to complete. You don't have much more time." I knew exactly what He was saying. It was clear. I've said this to a few people. The dog and I both knew in our spirits. No one, but us. And we sat and looked at each other quite often as if to say, "Is it me or is it you?" But we both know that it was one or both of us. The angel of death was very close.

Around mid-September, early October, I started experiencing sicknesses. Small things. My body began to exhibit one problem after the other. Up until that point, I was one of the healthiest patients over sixty that my doctor had. I wasn't on any regularly prescribed medications. I was the picture of good health. Getting regular physicals at least twice a year, never having any reasons to question that I would be around for a long time. But in October 2022, I received a message loud and clear that my time was short. I couldn't tell anybody, nor could I prove it. Just one of those things that you know. Then it was time for me to prepare, so I began to do just that, including and especially this writing this book.

Before moving on to the diagnosis, I've chosen three shortened versions of very long sermons that I have delivered or preached during my active ministry in Called and Chosen Ministries that I feel I should share. As I stated in the introduction of this book, the purpose of my writing is to help to develop a more spiritual relationship and less religious one in the reader, and to cause people to realize the sovereignty of God in all situations and circumstances.

## Nugget

I'm not one of them. I chose to leave the church with my spirituality intact.

It puzzles me to understand how biblical scholars and true students of the Word can twist and adulterate the Word of God to either fit their own agenda or conform to a clearly dysfunctional, pre-existing corrupted system. That, under the guise of religion, is called the church.

# Chapter 4

**Shortened versions of long sermons**

In reference to the sermons that I preached, I'm sure you will find much of what is written in the sermons in this book will bear some resemblance to sermons or parts of sermons that the reader may have heard preached by others. This is all due to the fact that many preachers throughout the years have preached on many of the same scriptures and come to many of the same conclusions, lessons, and sermons.

**Who are your battles with? Inward, outward, and upward by Darrel Johnson**

When we accepted Christ, we were born anew. Born again of the spirit. This was the initialization of the journey inward, outward, and upward toward spiritual maturity, toward self-realization, and toward the fulfillment of our earthly responsibilities as ambassadors for Christ. This journey is toward our true destiny. Where we would experience tests and trials that will stretch us to our very limits while building our faith and maturing us spiritually. The journey began inward, outward, and upward from the moment we became part of the body of Christ, the kingdom of God. While we were on this journey, we were in a state and place of constant warfare, spiritual warfare. We must never lose focus on the fact that it is spiritual warfare. If we take a moment to focus our attention on the journey inward, we will find that we must consider the question, who are our battles with?

The journey inward, who are our battles with?

Satan is real. He is truly evil and fully opposed to Christ. He came to kill, steal, and destroy and is diligently on the job. Satan wants to kill you in spirit, and in the process, kill your physical body. He wants to steal your peace, and in the process, cause you to lose your faith. He wants to destroy all that is good and pure, and in the process, destroy your covenant relationship with God. Anything to keep you from being holy. Satan's plan, if it succeeds, is to make you as you were when you didn't know Christ. Spiritually dead. Satan wants to cause a disconnect between you and God. Satan presents a constant state of hostility against anything that is Christ-like. Satan will use every trick he can to keep you from completing your journey. He has declared war on anything and everyone that is of God or represents the image of God. That would be you and I. As long as we are committed to spiritual growth and holiness, we are at war. It's biblical and it is our responsibility to be at war.

We are Christian soldiers. We are God's chosen. We are God's called. When did it feel like I was at war? It was probably because I was no threat to Satan. You see, this war is nothing new. Adam and Eve lost the first battle that man became involved in way back in the garden, when they allowed themselves to be tempted by the Enemy to give in to their own desires. I doubt that they felt like they were at war. It is key to recognize, and I reiterate, they gave in to their own desires. So, who was their primary battles with?

Allow me to clarify my position. Yes, we are exactly where we're supposed to be. While Satan continues to attempt to succeed at his evil intentions, we are to fight the good fight. Ephesians 6:10-12 KJV teaches, *Finally, my brethren, be strong in the Lord. And in the power of his might. Put on the whole armour of God, that ye may be able to stand against the wiles of the devil. For we wrestle not against flesh and blood, but against principalities, against powers, against the rulers of the darkness of this world, against spiritual wickedness in high places.* Spiritual wickedness in high places. Whose mate? His mate. Able to do what? Stand. You see, though we are at war, the battle is not ours, it's the Lords. Most of our battles are inward with ourselves, recognizing this as primary necessity in the process of continuing to fulfill our journey inward, outward, and upward toward our true destiny.

A war consists of many battles and skirmishes on many different fronts and stages. While we are currently at war, we already know the end results. That is fixed. Jesus has already defeated Satan. Stand strong in the fight. Fight the good fight. *Being confident of this, that he who has begun a good work in you will carry it on to completion until the day of Christ Jesus* (Phil. 1:6 NIV). We are encouraged. The fight is fixed. Satan has no power over us, us being those who have accepted Jesus Christ and given them control over our existence. So, who are your primary battles with?

## God Still Loves You
## by Darrel Johnson

Love is a many splendid thing. This is the title of an old song (though "splendid" is actually "splendored" in the title). I thought about that title and realized that I wasn't quite sure what splendid was. Some definitions of splendid include magnificent, gorgeous, sumptuous, exciting admiration by its fine or noble quality. So, I guessed that true love was a really many splendid thing.

We spend our lives looking for love, pursuing love. Longing for it. Thinking we can grasp it. We believe that we know what it means and how it works, but until we are fully led by the Spirit in our love affairs, we haven't really got a clue. If we want to even begin to understand the concept of love, you have to know God. God is love. Jesus teaches us that the greatest two commandments are, one, to love God with all your heart, with all your soul, and with all your mind., and the second is likened to the first, to love our neighbors as ourselves (Matt. 22:37-40). God's love is unconditional, not requiring that we earn it. We should not require that others earn ours.

We should set a goal of loving without conditional limitations. Living in the world is almost always conditional. Is almost always based on fulfilling the needs of one person. A worldly type of love is a love that will love you until your feelings are hurt, until you're spoken badly about, until you're lied to, until you're failed in some way. A worldly kind of love is a love that is grounded in selfish desires. A love that will only love you if you are fulfilling your desires when you need them met.

We see this worldly, shallow kind of love in youth. All of the time, we see girls who are young and so eagerly seeking for a guy to show them love, and that guy does show them love in the beginning, or something that resembles it. He takes them on dates. He writes them sweet love poems. He buys them flowers. She gets emotionally wrapped up in their relationship and begins to believe that they are in love. Then she has sex with him because he said, "If you love me, you'll do it." Once the self-desires have been fulfilled, he dumps her. I'm quite sure there's at least one person reading who not only knows what I'm talking about, but has also experienced this firsthand. Can you remember yourself saying to someone else or to yourself at least once in your life, "I really thought he or she loved me"? It's a hard lesson to learn. That worldly kind of love is a love that takes advantage of us.

God's love is totally the opposite. God's love, to me, is liberating. Accepting, forgiving, supporting, empowering, and completely unconditional, God's love just continues to give. You see, there's something else that we must realize from a worldly perspective. We certainly do not and did not deserve God's love. Let's go to 1 John 4:7-11. The word in the New International Version starting at verse 7, *Dear friends, let us love one another, for love comes from God.* Whoever does not love does not know God because God is love. This is how God showed His love among us. He sent His one and only Son into the world that we might live through Him. This is love. Not that we loved God, but He loved us and sent His Son as an atoning sacrifice for our sins. Dear friends, since God so loved us, we also want to love one another.

And now let's look back at Ephesians 3:17-19 (NIV). *So that Christ may dwell in your hearts through faith. And I pray that you, being rooted and established in love, may have power, together with all the Lord's holy people, to grasp how wide and long and high and deep is the love of Christ, and to know this love that surpasses knowledge-that you may be filled to the measure of all the fullness of God.* God's love is deep, and God's love has nothing to do with you. Others may love you, as in the introduction of this sermon, because you are fulfilling desires and needs or you might be a family. You might just be fun to be with. You might be eye candy. Handsome, pretty, cute, cuddly, or adorable. You might be rich. You might be the fulfillment of some desires that we don't necessarily need to touch on right now. I just hate going to maybe you have all of the qualities that fit someone's list. There could be a myriad of reasons why you could be experiencing a worldly type of love. There are many reasons why others love you, but not so with God. God loves you simply because He wants to love you. He chose you. He decided to love you. God loves you because God is love (1 John 4:16).

We're all familiar with all types of love through a worldly perspective. There's puppy love, grandparent love, first love, love for the arts, and love of food. I could go on and on. We throw that word around so quickly and easily. "I just love some of this" and "I just love some of that." We also have all types of friends. Fair weather friends, long distance friends, new friends, old friends, former friends, close friends. These are all components of a worldly, human weak love. Human love is crazy, sporadic, and unpredictable, often temporary, and almost always conditional. But God is love, and His love is unconditional, constant, and perfect. You can't influence God's love because God is love. Jesus didn't go to the cross because of any love you had for Him. He didn't go to the cross for any influence you placed on Him. *But God showed us his great love for us by sending Christ to die for us while we were still sinners* (Rom. 5:8 NLT). Jesus must have really loved you to do that for you because your sins put Him there. Jesus died the death of a sinner, though He was without sin. He took our sins upon Himself. He was the propitiation for our sins.

Sometimes people look at others. They have money, a good job, and good health. They live a good life. They have a good family and marriage and mistakenly think God must really love them. Look how much He has blessed them. Or at others in the reverse. They have problems. They are living badly. They are sick, poor, have lost their job, or are plagued with family or medical issues, trauma, and the mistaken perception is that God must not really love them. Look at the problems they have. That's nonsense. Circumstances have nothing to do with God's love. Even when everything seems to be going wrong, God's still loves you. When everything seems to be going right, God still loves you. If you want to gauge God's love, if you need a yardstick to measure His love, don't look at the circumstances, Look at the cross. Jeremiah 31:3 (NIV) says, *The Lord appeared to us in the past, saying: "I have loved you with an everlasting love. I have drawn you with unfailing kindness."* Remember in John 16:44, Jesus said, "*No man comes to me unless the Father who sent me draws them."* God drew you because He loves you immeasurably.

What do we need to do to experience God's love? Just receive it. Why? Because nothing can separate you from God's love. Let's go directly to the scripture lesson. Romans 8:31-39. When we look at verse 35, Paul asked the question, Who shall separate us from the love of Christ? Look at how Paul leads up to this statement in verse 28. We read the familiar passage, and we know that in all things, God works for the good of those who love Him, who are the called according to His purpose. This is a demonstration of God's love that all things, all circumstances, all problems, all blessings, everything that comes our way is an opportunity for God to demonstrate His love for us after touching on the doctrine of predestination.

In verses 29 and 30, Paul then gives us a series of questions leading up to verse 35. In verse 31 (NIV), he asks, *What, then, shall we say in response to these things? If God is for us, who can be against us?* Excellent question, one that we've probably asked in many situations and in many other ways. We may have asked with everybody and everything against us, where is God? We all face opposition, but if we weren't a threat to Satan, he wouldn't come against us. We face all types of opposition from our bodies (sickness, aches, and pain), from people hard to get along with (sometimes unlovable or those who will hurt your feelings, disappoint you), and from circumstances (things that don't go our way or the way we thought they would go). But Paul's question. What, then, can we say to these things as God's love in mind?

So, the question isn't, "How can I handle all that life throws at me?" The question is, "Can God handle all that life throws at me? Because if God is for us, who can be against us?" While we may have problems in life, God isn't fazed. God is greater than anything life throws at us. Is there a problem God can't handle? No. That's how much He loves us. How much He loves you. The question isn't *can* God handle my problems, but *will* God handle my problems? Paul answered that question in verse 32 (NIV). He said, *He who did not spare his own Son, but gave him up for us all-how will he not also, along with him, graciously give us all things?* God and His love gave you everything you need to meet life's problems. God loved you so much that He sent His Son to die on a cross for you. Jesus loves you so much that He was willing to die on the cross for you.

So, if God and Jesus loved you so much to do this for you, will they forget all about you in your time of need? No way. God has too much love vested in you to just walk off and forget about you now. We can all sing that song, "I Don't Believe He Brought Me This Far to Leave Me." But then we ask, How could God love me when I'm so unworthy of His love? He sees my life. He knows how I live. He knows me inside and out. He knows when I failed Him and failed to live up to His love. There's too much sin in my life for God to love someone like me. So, how could God love me?

Paul answers that with the next question. In verse 33, he says, Who is willing to bring any charge against those? Oh, God has chosen. It is God who justifies. Once God accepts you for who and what you are, and loves you anyhow, who else's opinion matters? People may criticize you, condemn you, gossip about you, cheat on you. Find fault and nitpick about you, berate or belittle you, and accuse you. The Word tells us the same as the accuser of the brethren. Revelation 12:10 even says that's exactly what Satan is doing right now, before God. Allow your imagination to go there.

Can you hear Satan saying, "Look at Darrel. Did you see what he did today? And look at Diane. Did you hear what she said? Did you tune into those thoughts that Darrel had when he got angry? And he calls himself a Christian and even a preacher, at that. That should show you how much He loves you and after all you've done for Him, that you've done for all of them"?

Now watch. God looks as Satan and says, "I'm sorry, but I don't see Diane and Darrel."

Satan replies, "Right down there, right there. You see them."

God answers, "Sorry, I don't see Diane and Darrel. I look upon them and all I see is my Son, Jesus. I see righteousness. I see some who have been justified by their faith. Justified by faith. Just as if I had never done it. Just as if it had never happened."

Let's always remember that God can use anyone in all different types of characters. We can remove the focus from ourselves and look at some biblical examples. Noah was a drunk. Jacob was a liar. Sampson was a womanizer. Rahab was a prostitute. David had an affair and was a murderer. Elijah was suicidal. Isaiah preached naked. Jonah ran from God. Peter denied Christ. The disciples fell asleep while praying. Who will bring any charge against those who God has chosen? It's God who justifies. In Colossians 1:28 (NIV), Paul says, *He is the one we proclaim, admonishing and teaching everyone with all wisdom, so that we may present everyone fully mature in Christ.*

So, let's read Romans 8:33 (NIV) again. *Who will bring any charge against those whom God has chosen? It is God who justifies.* God loves you so much. He doesn't hold your sin against you or condemn you. All He sees is His Son, Jesus, who justified you before the throne of grace. The word in Jeremiah 31:34 (NIV) says, "For I will forgive their wickedness and will remember their sins no more." God loves you so much that no one else's opinion matters but His. No one can sway God's opinion of you. Romans 8:34 tells us that Christ Jesus is at the right hand of God interceding for us.

And we're back to verse 35. Who shall separate us from the love of Christ? Shall trauma, trouble, hardship, persecution, famine, nakedness, danger, or sword? Now, the big question of the day. If any of those things comes your way, does it mean God does not have love for you? No. Verse 37 (NIV) says, *in all these things we are more than conquerors through him who loved us.* Nothing can drive a wedge between you and God's love for you.

Still not convinced? Let's look at Romans 8:38-39 (NIV). *For I am convinced that neither death nor life, neither angels nor demons, neither the present nor the future, nor any powers, neither height nor depth, nor anything else in creation, in all creation, will be able to separate us from the love of God that is in Christ Jesus our Lord.* Paul was persuaded, convinced beyond a shadow of a doubt. None of the circumstances mentioned here, or any other circumstances, can separate you from God's love. Of this, we, too, can also be convinced. You have never lived a day, a minute, a second when God didn't love you.

You may have hidden from God like Adam and Eve in the garden of Eden, but God still loves you. You may have deserted Him like the disciples when they fled when Jesus was arrested. But God still loves you. You may have denied Him like Peter when they asked about the relationship with Jesus Christ, but God still loves you. You may have doubted Him like Thomas when he was told that Jesus had risen. He didn't believe. He said he needed proof, but God still loves you. In it all, through thick and thin, good times and bad times, God still loves you. You never leave His mind, His thoughts, or His sight. He sees in you and loves you anyhow.

Jeremiah 31:3 (NIV) says, *"I have loved you with an everlasting love; I have drawn you with unfailing kindness."*

When you sit at the bedside of a loved one who has racked in pain or disease, God still loves you. When you sit at the graveside after losing one who has touched your heart in life, God still loves you. When you weep because your financial burdens seem too heavy to bear, God still loves you. When you see your family torn apart or a marriage heading for disaster, God still loves you. When your heart aches because of a great sin you've committed and you feel that God could never forgive you, God still loves you. When you're faced with the many trials and tribulations of this journey throughout life, God still loves you.

God could never love you anymore than He already does and God could never love you any less than He already does. You can't get any more of God's love because God is love. We think that God would love us more if we cursed less, drank less, sinned less. We think that God will love us more if we pray more, study the Bible more, and attend church more. Live a better life. While these things are our responsibility to continue to do our best to achieve and succeed at, these things are certainly an indicator of our love for God, but they don't impact or change God's love for us one bit.

What am I saying? The last verse of scripture, Romans 8:39 (NIV), *neither height nor depth, nor anything else in all creation, will be able to separate us from the love of God that is in Christ Jesus our Lord.* God's love isn't based on you. It's based on Jesus, which is in Christ Jesus. Our Lord God will always love you as much as He loves His Son, Jesus, because you are in Christ. Are you experiencing God's love? For you, is it real to you? God has poured out His love into our hearts by the Holy Spirit (Rom. 5:5). He is given unto you so that you have the capacity to know, feel joy, and experience God's love. How? Because the Holy Spirit dwells within you.

Let God's love permeate your life. Wake up in the morning and bask in the sunshine of His love. Go to bed at night and rest in the comfort of His love. Live in His love. Immerse yourself in His love. Fill your life with His love. Let His love overpower you. Let His love surround you, and let all who look upon you see and experience God's love. Never forget John 3:16 (KJV), *For God so loved the world, that he gave his only begotten Son, that whosoever believeth in him should not perish, but have everlasting life.* That's love. God still loves you.

Let me tell you about God's love. I've heard it said this way many times, in many different ways. Do you know Him today? Do you know His love for His creation? He supplies strength for the week. He's available for the tempted in the tribe. He sympathizes and saves. He strengthens and sustains. He guards and he guides. He heals the sick. He forgives sinners. He discharges debtors. He delivers the captives. He defends the feeble. He blesses the young. He serves the unfortunate. He regards the agent. He rewards the diligent. He beautifies the meager. Do you really know our Father? Our God is the key to knowledge. He's the wellspring of wisdom. He's a doorway of delivery. He's a pathway of peace. He's a roadway of righteousness. He's a highway of holiness. He's a gateway of glory. There's no way to measure His limitless love. He's enduringly strong. He's entirely sincere. He's eternally steadfast. He's immortally graceful. He's imperially powerful. He's impartially merciful. I could keep talking about how much God loves you. He really knows His love and what He did. He sent His only begotten Son whose life is matchless. His goodness is limitless. His mercy is everlasting. His love never changes. His word is enough. His grace is sufficient. His reign is righteous, His yoke is easy, and His burden is light. I'm trying to tell you about His love for you.

So, you know and understand God and His love, but you see, you can never fully, completely explain God and His love. He's incomprehensible. He's invincible. He's irresistible. You can't get Him out of your mind, and you can't get Him off of your hands. You can't live without Him, and you can't outlive Him. The Pharisees couldn't stand Him. They found out they couldn't stop Him. Pilot couldn't find fault in Him, and Herod couldn't kill Him. Death couldn't handle Him, and the grave couldn't hold Him. And all of His magnificent glory, with all of these attributes and qualities, God still loves you.

## Break Free
## by Darrel Johnson

This particular sermon was preached as Part 3 to a prayer breakfast/brunch given by Carlton Chosen Ministries. The prayer breakfast was given a theme of "Breakthrough, Break Fast, and Break Free." "Breakthrough" was a word delivered by Sister Felicia McCoy, "Break Fast" was presented by Sister J. Vizzini, and "Break Free," the final sermon, fell on me. The interesting part of this while applying hindsight being 20/20 vision is that it wasn't just my assignment for the day, but a lifelong assignment.

I began the sermon with the familiar phrase that I often shared. "Don't go by what I say, but verify it for yourselves." God doesn't want you to just believe every word that precedes from a preacher's mouth. God wants you to go to His Word. Psalm 19:105 reminds us that God's word is a lamp unto our feet and a light unto our path. Jesus reiterates it in John 6:45 (NLT), he said, *It is written in the Scriptures, 'They will all be taught by God.' Everyone who listens to the Father and learns from him comes to me.* I have been fully aware of my assignments since the day I accepted my call. Truth be told, as it is written in the Word in many places (specifically in the Old Testament books of Isaiah and Jeremiah), we all have the same assignment. God said to Jeremiah in chapter 1, verse 5 (NLT), *"I knew you before I formed you in your mother's womb. Before you were born, I set you apart and appointed you as my prophet to the nations."* Isaiah 49:5 speaks of the fact that God had been his strength, that God formed him in his mother's womb to be His servant. That God commissioned him in order to bring His people, Israel, back to Himself. This is not just an assignment for Isaiah and Jeremiah, but for all of us. You see, God has had this plan from the very beginning. It has all been laid out. Each of us has been called.

Look at what Jesus tells us in the New Testament, John 6:44. He says, "No one can come to me unless the Father who sent me draws him." That's the scripture that God gave me for my next sermon. It also brings me to the first point of today. We were first led by the Spirit. This means that we are to continue to be led by the Spirit. We are each and every one of us called of God to a relationship with our Lord and Savior, Jesus the Christ. What, do you say, does this have to do with break free? I'm going to tell you.

First, I must say do not use the words break free conjunctively in the same as. You could say breakthrough describing something you experienced or have. The act of breaking through some sort of resistance. You do not use it in the same way as when you say the word breakfast. In describing a meal or an act of actually getting breakfast or breaking a fast. We have to use it as two separate distinctive words, break and free. Let's look at the scriptures for that theme. Galatians 5:1 (NIV) states. *It is for freedom that Christ has set us free. Stand firm, then, and do not let yourselves be burdened again by the yoke of slavery.* Then we go to John 8:36, which reminds us that if the Son sets you free, you will be free indeed.

Since freedom is the key here, we'll examine what it means to be free. Some of the definitions that Webster [3] describes for free are not in bondage. Not under the control of some person or arbitrary power. Able to act or think without compulsion or arbitrary restriction. Having liberty to be able to move in any direction. Not held as in chains. Not held or burdened by obligations, debts, discomforts, etc. Unhindered, not held or confined by prejudice or bias. The list goes on and on.

Before I go any further, I would like to plant this one question in your conscious thought so that you might refer to it regularly from this point on. And the second point I'd like to make is you must be free to be spirit led. Examine the definitions that I just shared with you and ask yourself, am I free? Ask yourself, are my decisions and actions spirit *led*, or are they first filtered through the control of some other person or some arbitrary worldly power? In the body of Christ, is my ministry restricted by some rules made by men? Look at Mark 7:5-9 (NIV) and ask yourself, am I free? Jesus, in response to the Pharisees and teachers when they asked him why His disciples didn't follow the traditions of the elders, put it this way. *"The people honor me with their lips, but their hearts are far from me. They worship me in vain; their teachings are merely human rules. You have let go of the commands of God and are holding on to human traditions. You have a fine way of setting aside the commands of God in order to observe your own traditions!"*

You see, they weren't free, and neither were the people who followed them. Jesus said this to the religious leaders, and through His word ,hH echoes it through the centuries. It is obvious that neither Jesus nor I am suggesting that we do not conform to the

---

[3] *Merriam-Webster.com Dictionary*, s.v. "freedom," accessed July 24, 2023, https://www.merriam-webster.com/dictionary/freedom.

godly standards set forth, or that we don't respect God's given authority. What is being taught here is that we discern the difference between godly authority and worldly authority and make decisions accordingly. Garlic character will always be apparent in every situation.

Am I free? You must be free to be spirit led. Am I allowing my God-given liberty to function in my call and fulfill my purpose to be obscured by some already existing dysfunctional system that has been so infiltrated by worldly tactics and principles that it trump's the kingdom of God so that the world can't see that it is here? Let's be real. God does not need us to be kingdom builders. The kingdom of God already exists. The kingdom of God is here and now. It is our responsibility to, through the ability to call on the power of the Holy Spirit, be the physical manifestation of the already existing spiritual kingdom of God. We can't do that if we give up our freedom. We can't do that if we are not led by the Spirit.

Are we free? Am I free to be the example that God has called me to be? Am I free to create? Exercise true religion and worship. No more jumping through man-made hoops that had very little to do with the will of God. Man-made hoops that are only set in place to foster and build man's temporal kingdom here on Earth. True religion is here to quicken you and mature you spiritually, mentally, and physically. Our faith and our religion is part of a process that God is using to prepare us and others through our witness and ministry for a higher level of existence. Jumping through man-made hoops replaces His spirituality. For a foolish culture of form and fashion, He gives the Antichrist a stronghold in the church and helps to conceal the kingdom of God from the secular world. Calling ourselves Christians does not. We cannot limit ourselves only to being Christians on Sundays or while in the presence of our contemporaries. Christianity is a full-time responsibility.

On your job and in every aspect of your life, look at some of your situations and circumstances, some of the powerlessness that we portray to the world for all of the wrong reasons. Are we holding on to relationships, situations, and circumstances that are unhealthy for us mentally, physically, and spiritually? Maybe there are some habits and ways within us that must be addressed. These things are hindering us from reaching the level of spiritual maturity that God is trying to bring us to. I'm not just referring to private, interpersonal relationships and situations. I'm talking about any and all nonproductive, hindering, controlling, manipulative, abusive, toxic, ungodly relationships, situations, actions, and habits. These are the things that keep us from being free, anything that is counterproductive for the representation of the kingdom of God.

In order for us to be free, in order for us to be truly led by the Spirit, something must be broken. This is my third and final point. We have to break some things. What does Webster say about break?[4] He says to create failure by force to make unusable or inoperative by cracking, disrupting, etc. To tame, to make obedient. With or as with force. To get rid of, to escape from by force, to bring to a certain end.

The operative word here is force. We have to break some things with force or power. How do we do that, you ask? With the power of the Holy Spirit. Yes, we have to break free in order to be free, and to be led by the Spirit, we need to break free from anything that hinders us. To break free from our own hindrances like pride and conceit, we need to break free from disobedience and lust. We need to break free from ungratefulness and unholiness. We need to break free from hindrances imposed upon us by false teachers.

---

[4] *Merriam-Webster.com Dictionary*, s.v. "break," accessed July 24, 2023, https://www.merriam-webster.com/dictionary/break.

We need to break free from the bondage resulting from the abuse of spiritual authority. By our leaders, we need to break free from the effects of false faith that has become toxic in many instances of faith that is placed in people and institutions of faith placed in pre-existing dysfunctional systems.

If you are in a place or situation where God is telling you to break free, today is the day. We have to have faith in the Holy Spirit and confidence in ourselves to use the power that we have to call upon the Holy Spirit to empower us to break free. Acts 3:1-11 speaks about how Peter healed the crippled beggar. Peter in verse 6 of that particular pericope of scripture, operating in the power of the Holy Spirit, said, "In the name of Jesus Christ of Nazareth, rise up and walk." Peter said this with boldness and confidence. Rise up and walk. He didn't stutter. He didn't wait for a sign from heaven. He didn't wait for an affirmation from men. He straightforwardly commanded the man to rise up and walk.

What commands are we making in the name of Jesus Christ in order to break free from our situations? Are we commanding our peace, our healing, our deliverance? Are we speaking in boldness over our families? Of our situations at work, at home, and in the churches and in the communities? Are we speaking with boldness? It's time for a breakthrough. We are led by the Spirit, and today's the day that we break free.

## Nugget

Spiritual revelation. A lesson/message poured into my spirit by God the day after there was a torrential rainstorm in my area.

Nothing exists without water. Life is renewed by and created in water. Without water, everything on this great big planet Earth would cease to exist. A seed must wither, die, and fall to the ground only to dry up without water, never to spring forth new life. Newborn babies are conceived, then develop in an embryonic sack (mostly water) where they develop enough to exist in the outside world. Likewise, seeds are buried in moist soil, watered regularly to develop roots, a strong foundation, and a method to transfer water and nutrients absorbed from the soil through its system before springing forth to the outside world. Bring in what we see as new life and beauty with purpose.

Like the seed, when I die, my spiritual seed, planted by God will be fed by the living water. I will spring forth in a beautiful spirit to a higher level of existence. ~Darrel Johnson

> *But whosoever drinketh of the water that I shall gave him shall never thirst; but the water that I shall give him shall be in him a well of water springing up into everlasting life.* John 4:14 (KJV)

# Chapter 5

The good Lord has blessed me in so many ways throughout my life, and up until now, He has blessed me and used me to be a blessing to many. Even when I did not see it, He was using me. Thank God I'm able to look back and see how He's accomplished these things. Even in the trials and tribulations, I can see the blessings. He shows me that my living has not been in vain. As I share my testimony with others–friends, neighbors, contemporaries, and family–they usually respond by telling me the ways that God has touched their lives through using me. I see things I would never have imagined were happening. In most cases, this is also a blessing and a gift from God. I also thank God for the advanced notice, an opportunity for preparation, not just to prepare myself for the outcome, but to prepare my family, friends, and loved ones. God has instructed me to present this message to the world.

As I said in my introduction, I've had a truly blessed life. I've been there, done that, and I won't take nothing for my journey now. I know that I know that He didn't bring me this far to leave me. So, I'm prepared to move on and be with Him, on to that higher level of existence in glory. So, here's where we are now and how we got here. The sickness, the process, the diagnosis, and the prognosis.

As I wrote earlier in the book, it was back around June or July of 2022 when I had the epiphany, God had clearly told me my time was short. He did not tell me how short, but He did make it clear that I needed to finish the work that He had instructed me to start. Within the next three months, especially after I started developing little sicknesses and issues with my health, I came to a point of acceptance and peace. That's when I began to pray a prayer that was very similar to the prayer that Jesus prayed at the garden of Gethsemane (I paraphrase). "Father, if You could take this cup from me, please do, but if not, I'm good with it. I trust You, Lord. Nevertheless, not my will, but thy will be done."

The sickness first presented itself in mid-October as a mild pain in my chest and a spike in my blood pressure, which sent me to an urgent care center. They, in turn, instructed me to go to an emergency room. I went to Saint Agnes Hospital. There, they did all of the routine tests they go through when a patient is present with chest pains, including a CAT scan. They diagnosed me with inflammation of the pancreas, fatty liver, and emphysema. I was sent home with instructions to lose weight, avoid fatty foods and alcohol. I also found in my documentation through some miscommunication there was a diagnosis of excessive alcohol use (ETOH). I quickly corrected that, at least I thought I did. The same problems continued, along with the same symptoms.

About a month later, I went to my primary care physician, who ordered another CAT scan. This was mid-November. When she reviewed the results, she diagnosed me with acute pancreatitis and instructed me to immediately go to the emergency room. Back to Saint Agnes I went. There, they did another CAT scan, kept me overnight, and ran all of the same routine tests. They downgraded my diagnosis to mild inflammation of the pancreas, fatty liver, and emphysema.

I then went to individual specialists. The gastroenterologist did an endoscopy and determined that my pancreas was not the problem. The pulmonologist did all of his tests and determined that my lungs were not the issue. The hepatologist determined that my liver and associated blood work were relatively normal and not the issue. I was still experiencing the pain, which increased progressively over time. It seemed that the professionals at Saint Agnes gave up on trying to diagnose the cause of the problem and decided to treat the symptoms, which was my pain. So now, I was seeing a pain specialist. The pain specialist put me on an interesting cocktail of Gabapentin and Tramadol. Both of these drugs caused a lot of side effects that affected my digestive system and my physical condition extremely.

By now, I had lost over forty pounds and was still losing weight and having difficulty managing the pain. The symptoms were indicative of one of two things, either internal shingles attacking my celiac ganglion nerve bundle or some type of cancer or growth pressing on those same nerves. By the middle of March 2023, while suffering through the undiagnosed issues and pain for six months now, my primary care physician sent me a letter telling me that she would no longer treat me, that she was changing her practice, and I needed to choose another doctor.

I signed myself into a new service, a concierge service with a wonderful doctor who ordered another CAT scan. By this time, I was so sick that I was sure that whatever was going on inside of me would certainly kill me very soon. In fact, the morning that my doctor was going to call me and suggest that I go to the emergency room, I beat him to the punch. I called him and told him that's what my plans were, and he instructed me to go to Johns Hopkins Emergency Room.

At Johns Hopkins, they did all of the same tests and scans as required. They also did an ERCP, which is a more thorough scan of my pancreas and digestive system. They found a large mass growing on the head of my pancreas. They did biopsies and told me that the results would be received within seven to ten days. I knew the results immediately because God had already informed me my time was short. I was already prepared, both mentally and spiritually.

It was very interesting while I was there in the hospital before they discharged me. The way that they tried to gently prepare me for what they had a good idea was coming. Doctors would come into my room and have these hypothetical conversations with me. Asking me questions like, "If this is possibly cancer, would you be open to and willing to subject yourself to studies and trials and research?" While they were talking, in my imagination, they were looking like wolves drooling at their mouths. I know that what they saw was a prime candidate for their research and their studies.

They discharged me two days after the ERCP test, or eight days before the projected results. One of the doctors from the oncology team met me at the elevator on my way to catch my Uber. She said, "Mr. Johnson, we don't have the complete results, but we do have preliminary results of your biopsies. It is cancer and the cancer is malignant."

My response was simply, "Thank you. May I still go home?"

The ride home from the hospital was a particularly trying one. How would I tell my wife? Not that I hadn't been avoiding that from the start, but I had to tell her because I was sure I had pancreatic cancer. The monster of cancer diagnosis's, the diagnosis that is usually a death sentence. Because of my epiphany, I had been doing research the whole time. I knew that this type of cancer was not usually caught until it was in stage 4 and that by the time that it was in stage 4, that life expectancy was generally less than three years and oftentimes only a few months.

April 11th was the date set to meet with the oncology team and find out the exact findings of the biopsies. The prognosis, again, I already knew. Not that I was looking at things from a negative perspective, but I was looking at things from a spiritual perspective. God was very clear to me. So, when I found out that it was stage 4 and that it had metastasized into my lung and liver, I was not surprised. The spots that Saint Agnes had diagnosed as emphysema and fatty liver were the cancer that was already developing on both of those organs. The ERCP findings just confirmed it all.

Before I go any further, let me share with you and remind you of my mindset and my faith level before that and at that point. I've never been afraid of death. I've always known we're all going to do it, we just don't know when. My thoughts were, *I just don't want it to hurt.* I used to say things like, "I'm going to go out like Enoch." He did not know death. With that said, looking into the future, anything's possible and God is in control. I do believe in miracles. So, back to my prayer. "Lord, if you could take this cup from me, it would be nice, but if You should choose not to, I'll understand. Nevertheless, not my will, but Your will be done. I would like to be around long enough to see my grandchildren grow into mature adults."

As I was saying, I came home from the hospital that evening with my grab the bull by the horns attitude. Let's take this fight on with everything that we have and kick its ass. At the same time, the doctors who happened to have been drooling at the mouth knowing that I was a prime candidate for their clinical trials, these same doctors who were willing to take a 50/50 gamble on my life were busy scheduling those tests and biopsies. They did this before I gave them a "yes or no" answer. Before I answered them or signed any documentation, they were just going ahead with their plans. Thank God for discernment and a reasonable amount of knowledge, luckily for me. I advocate for myself. I'm very thorough in looking at my records and files and I caught it all the same night.

By the next morning, I was correcting those issues and canceling those appointments. I got a lot of clarification phone calls from people who needed to make or set the record straight with questions like, "Let me understand, did you not approve this?" I'm sure that a lot of people faced a lot of trouble and are all still hoping not to catch flak because of it. I, on the other hand, am just hoping to continue to get the best treatment while at the same time trusting that God is in control and that life is unfolding as it should. After my first round of chemotherapy, the doctors realized that my pancreas was not functioning as it should. They brought me back in for more testing. They scheduled another ERCP. They found that the original stent that they implanted was not functioning correctly and that I wasn't able to digest food properly. So, they replaced it with a new stent, a better stent.

A friend of mine introduced me to someone who introduced me to a holistic treatment that Doctor Sebi had prescribed in the past to treat different types of cancers. This was a controversial treatment, but I was willing to try it. That and because I wasn't able to take on any nutrients. By now, I had lost over seventy pounds. The second ERCP was performed, the original stent was replaced with a new stent, and my pancreas and my body began to function somewhat. I did get an opportunity to try the holistic herbal treatments, but my body reacted very badly to this.

Neither I nor the doctors expected me to be around much longer. But God! The fact that I was still here by the middle of May was a miracle in itself. That's when I posted my first miracle report on Facebook, but God in the middle of June allowed me to issue my second miracle report. By now, you know where I'm going. If you look at the statistics, I am a statistical anomaly considering the condition they found me in back in March, and the yet unspoken prognosis of the medical professionals. Again, I say, but God.

So, here we are, going into July, and I'm in the process of finishing this book. Today is July 3. I have an appointment for July 6 when they will do the necessary tests and scans to determine whether or not the chemotherapy is working, or if we need to shift gears and try a new treatment plan. Due to the fact that I don't know what tomorrow holds, I am submitting this manuscript to my publisher now. Only God knows what tomorrow holds. So, we wait in faith to see what the Lord does. We hold on to the hope of miraculous healing.

This book is a testimony to the miracles of God, to His sovereignty in every life. The past three months have been a roller coaster of ups and downs and pains and struggles. Nights when I didn't think I would make it through the night, and days when I thought I would be okay forever. Everything I do, wondering if this is the last time that I'll get an opportunity to do this. I can't tell you what the future holds, but I can tell you that even through it all, each time I talk with or minister to family, friends, loved ones, and strangers, God uses the examples of my faith for others the same way He used the faith of the woman in the flowing white dress for me. Thank you, Father. God allows me to see that lives are being touched and that seeds are being planted. God allows me to see that my living is not and has not been in vain. What a blessing. So, back to my prayer. "Lord, if you could take this cup away from me, please do."

I would be remiss if I don't take a moment to thank my beautiful, lovely, amazing wife Diane for her strength, support, and love as she suffers through the trials with me. I love you. Thank you!

# Conclusion

As a child living at home with my mom and dad, in the bathroom hung on the wall was this poem. It had a title "Desiderata." At the bottom, it read. "Author unknown." I read it regularly and pondered very deeply on its words. Often during my youth, I thought that I was an atheist. I viewed the church and religion as some kind of crutch or club that people felt the need to belong to.

At the same time, the words of these writings resonated so deep within my being that I guess I could say that this was my Bible at the time. I aspired to follow it as admonishment on how to live well. I later came to realize that this was just one of the many seeds that God had planted and planned in the beginning of a long process of fulfilling His plan to draw me to a right relationship with Him and use me to minister to, and as a witness to the world that He is with us always and in **ALL THINGS.**

I've heard the word Bible be used as an acronym "**B. I. B. L. E.**" Basic Instruction Before Leaving Earth.

I admonish you to receive these writings into your spirit regardless of what you believe!

With love, **Darrel**

## Desiderata reads as follows:

Go placidly amid the noise and the haste, and remember what peace there may be in silence. As far as possible, without surrender be on good terms with all persons.

Speak your truth quietly and clearly, and listen to others, even the dull and the ignorant; they, too, have their story.

Avoid loud and aggressive persons; they are vexatious to the Spirit. If you compare yourself to others, you may become vain or bitter, for always there would be greater and lesser persons than yourself.

Enjoy your achievements as well as your plans, keep interested in your own career, however humble; it is a real possession in the changing fortunes of time.

Exercise caution in all your business affairs, for the world is full of trickery. But let this not blind you to what virtue there is; many persons strive for high ideals, and everywhere life is full of heroism.

Be yourself. Especially do not feign affection neither be cynical about love; for in the face of all aridity and disenchantment, it is as perennial as the grass.

Take kindly the Council of the years, gracefully surrendering the things of youth.

Nurture strength of spirit to shield you in sudden misfortune. But do not distress yourself with dark imaginings. Many fears are born of fatigue and loneliness.

Beyond a wholesome discipline, be gentle with yourself. You are a child of the universe no less than the trees and the stars; you have a right to be here.

And whether or not it is clear to you, no doubt the universe is unfolding as it should. Therefore, be at peace with God, whatever you conceive Him to be, and whatever your laborers and aspirations in the noisy confusion of life, Keep peace in your soul. With all its sham drudgery and broken dreams, it is still a beautiful world. Be cheerful. Strive to be happy.

Later research has found that this poem was written by Max Erman in 1927.

Ancient and Accepted Scottish Rite of Freemasonry
Valley of Baltimore, Orient of Maryland
Ill, Edward B Kraft, 33-degree Memorial Class
Spring 2015

Printed in the USA
CPSIA information can be obtained
at www.ICGtesting.com
LVHW012111250823
756294LV00009B/131